VEGETATION UNDER POWER
HEAT! BREATH! GROWTH!

T0016226

SPECTOR BOOKS

CONTENTS

Vegetation under Power
Heat! Breath! Growth!

Bauhaus Lab 2021

Since its foundation in 1892, the Kreismuseum Bitterfeld has focused intensively on documenting, preserving and conveying the heritage of the region's flora and fauna. This may be related to the passion of the museum's founder, Emil Obst, for the geological and scenic particularities of his homeland. But this historic narrative, which continues to inform the museum today, likewise evokes a certain degree of wonder at the radical changes which occurred in the landscape around Bitterfeld over the course of the twentieth century.

After all, the landscape of Central Germany rapidly changed from a rural to an industrial one in just a few decades. The industries were responsible for the production of fertilisers, explosives, chloric gas, etc., which boosted the demand for electrical energy and fossil fuels in the respective political regimes. These earthbound terrestrial transformations–from the landscapes torn up in the hunger for coal to the artificial lake areas created following the depletion of coal resources as part of an 'environmental structural change'–have led to a permanent reorganisation of the relationship structures of 'sociotechnical arrangements' (Bruno Latour) in the region and yielded an almost entirely manmade, anthropocentric landscape.

One silent witness to this terrestrial transformation is the herbarium of the botanist Hans Weber, dating 1931, which is kept in the museum. This formed the point of departure for the multidisciplinary research of the Bauhaus Lab 2021. The collection is also thought to be associated with the public debates about air pollution which were provoked by the rapid growth of industry. Among the documents in Bitterfeld's archives are citizens' complaints about, for instance, the autumnal appearance of trees and bushes in summer.

But the dried, pressed plants are not only silent witnesses to the lost vegetation of a damaged ecosystem; they also tell us about specific techniques of modern knowledge systems. In modern epistemology, nature was regarded as something external, to be collected, mapped, sorted and catalogued. In this sense, the practice of botanising and the forms of display derived therefrom found in the museum are related to the encounters with natural phenomena made by artists and designers at the historic Bauhaus. New media such as film and photography contributed to the fact that dialogues concerning the shift in the perception of the organic evolved in and around biology, philosophy and art. For the Bauhauslers, the camera served less as a means of representing plants and more as a new medium which revealed hitherto inaccessible insights. Karl Blossfeldt's *Art Forms in Nature,* a collection of photographs of plant forms associated with New Objectivity *(Neue Sachlichkeit)* that were exhibited at the Bauhaus Dessau in 1929, must be considered in the context of a new visual regime heralded by the new media and instruments such as microscopy and radiography. The limits of the visible were radically extended. Not only the phenomena of nature, but also their processuality and inherent homogeneity, could now be tapped. With the aid of the new imaging processes, silent nature could be 'given a voice'. In 1927, László Moholy-Nagy pointed out that the first modern media such as photography and film rendered visible this 'life force' which was imperceptible to the naked eye. In this, the Bauhauslers were inspired by the work of the biologist and cultural philosopher Raoul H. Francé, which posits biological functional sequences and energetic principles of design mediating between technology, the natural sciences and life. In association with new scientific visualisation technologies that also appealed to a wide audience in popular formats such as the 1926 film *Blumenwunder,* an idea of balancing spheres previously perceived as separate, such as nature and technology, took shape.

In the Bauhaus Lab 2021, the eight international participants pursued these perfunctory historic traces of the modern 'plant discipline' at the museum in Bitterfeld and the Bauhaus Dessau, and developed them further from multiple perspectives. Based on museum artefacts, materials, documents, photographs and personal testimonies, they developed narratives that do not pursue linearity or chronology as much as they propose different and contrasting means of describing the formation of societal nature-culture relationships. The arts and design research projects were motivated by how these articulate themselves in air movements, sedimentations in earth and water, fauna and flora, everyday culture, memories, institutional practices and image production. The focus rested on the concepts and ideologies of environment, nature, soil, ecology and sustainability, on the regulations, processes and methods that permeate these discourses which have materialised in the soil, vegetation, landscape and water. In this respect, the Lab was literally an attempt to 'earth' knowledge and to inspire ideas for a different approach to shaping a new nature-culture that encourages not only conservation and protection, but also healing and stewardship, and finds expression in new forms of solidarity with the environment and other species.

Regina Bittner

A black box in the archives of the Kreismuseum Bitterfeld contains a herbarium of leaves preserved from 1931. Created by the botanist Hans Weber, this collection is an inventory of flora gathered in the forest area of the Goitzsche. Opening this black box has been an invitation to understand the complex entanglements of human and non-human actors, technologies, material flows, socialities and moral orders that engulf this object and the landscape of Bitterfeld.

Throughout the twentieth century, this area underwent drastic transformations driven by the rapid development of opencast brown coal mines, the erection of power plants and the proliferation of chemical factories. The excavation and monumental movement of soil, the redirection of rivers and relocation of villages, the chemical alteration of ground, air and water, and, the radical impacts of these processes on the region's vegetal and animal life did not go unnoticed: They were accompanied by various institutional and citizen-led practices of care.

Could the herbarium, then, be a catalyst for research questioning the role of plants in the development of infrastructures and practices of care? Plants, after all, dwell within conditions of possibility and their emergent limits. If they provide new directions to explore the dialectical relationship between ecology and economy, our research suggests that vegetation be considered as the foundation of energy, yet also subjugated to different forms of power.

From the vantage point of the Bauhaus Building in Dessau, this research is inevitably entangled with the school's modernist legacies. Through artistic and design interventions in dialogue with archival material and testimonies, it proposed a new interpretation of the modernist motto 'Light! Air! Sun!' to 'Heat! Breath! Growth!' If 'heat' conveys the necessity of warming the home, it also reveals the pitfalls of extraction, industrialisation and its consequent environmental toxicities. Similarly, the seeming triviality of 'breath' is juxtaposed with the struggle for clean air, water and other resources, while the need for 'growth' – of plants, animals and the ecosystem writ large – is also challenged by linear narratives of unabashed progress. Such a lens provides an alternative view to the 'cleanliness' of modernism, focusing instead on its dirtier underbellies. In such a framework, nature does not exist outside the history of modernism but is an integral component from which Bitterfeld's landscapes are re-investigated in all their complex modalities.

The Bauhaus Lab 2021 focused on speculative futures and lost narratives that decentred anthropocentric histories to pose the following questions: How do we maintain and continue to care for landscapes that have been deemed beyond repair? What does it mean to care, or take care, in postindustrial landscapes? What are the histories of stewardship and activism that inform methods of repair and care?

Exhibition

Vegetation under Power / Heat! Breath! Growth!
Presented in: Bauhaus Dessau, Kreismuseum Bitterfeld
Bauhaus Lab 2021

Entwurzelungen
Wohin ziehen die Bäume?

Nature / Culture

As a curator working at the intersection of art and the environment, I ask myself: How do we encounter climate breakdown? Such a question is difficult to fully grasp, and the answer depends entirely on who we are and where we are, whether we exist on the frontline of environmental crises or experience them from a privileged distance.

Having been given a number of artifacts to respond to, it became clear to me that the question of time is of crucial importance, especially in order to make sense of how more-than-human beings may experience time at vastly different scales. The notion of relative time brings us into a completely different realm of ethics and relationships with the more-than-human world of plants, animals and mineral matter. So what are the temporalities that emerge from these artifacts, and what can they teach us?

Take, for instance, a piece of lignite. This in itself may contain remains of a bald cypress or a sequoia tree and can be as much as sixty-five million years old. It is an object that essentially holds deep time within itself, showing us an experience of time that is completely different from the one that we are familiar with.

If we then think about the amount of time it takes to burn a piece of coal such as lignite, say around twenty minutes, we begin to experience a dissonance between vastly incompatible scales, much in the same way that we might experience environmental catastrophes. A wildfire can devastate a hundred-year-old forest in a matter of minutes.

By observing this object, a composition of dead matter, we are simultaneously confronted with the acceleration of the experience of time in relation to its incineration, and deep time in the way it was formed. This is highly indicative of the way in which the Anthropocene paradigm works. After all, over the last few centuries we have managed to transform Earth at a greater-than-geological scale and speed.

One of the potentials of art and culture is how they help us enact or embody those shifts of perspective that can bring us closer to encountering climate breakdown, encountering the planet or encountering a more-than-human paradigm. To assume that the more-than-human world has agency is to understand polyphony as a way of experiencing both deep and shallow time simultaneously and as mutually interdependent.

Lucia Pietroiusti [1]

1 Guest speaker at the Bauhaus Lab 2021 International Symposium, 9 Dec., 2021, the following text is an adaptation of her presentation. Lucia Pietroiusti is a curator working at the intersection of art, ecology, and systems. She is also the founder of the General Ecology project at Serpentine London.

A geological map of Bitterfeld dated 1938 is scattered with small red dots, each one marking the site of a borehole drilled to gauge the mineral makeup of the ground. The map-makers were searching for lignite; their purpose, extraction. The borehole samples were diagrammed into clearly demar-cated mineral groups: clay, alluvial silts, brown coal, sand. Their naming rendered these different samples knowable while their classification made them commensurable. Under a geological gaze, these grounds ceased being places with more-than-human histories, ecologies and cultures. They became a resource.

As Bitterfeld's lignite fuelled its manufacturing and elec-trochemical industries, its landscapes were remade anew, successively becoming open cast lignite mines, industrial dumps, reclaimed land and recreational lakes. Standing on the recently restored datum of the shore of the Goitzsche, a visitor would be hard-pressed to know, first-hand, that this ground was once a forest, then a mine. The only tangible frag-ments of its material history that remain are held in the collec-tion of the Kreismuseum Bitterfeld.

What is most striking about viewing and handling the samples of lignite dug up almost a century ago is their heterogeneity. One sample is a piece of carbonised trunk from a once living, ancient tree, one of the many species that 8000 years ago inhabited the land which Bitterfeld now occupies. Another is a fragile and fragmented collection of semi-fossilised leaves, each a different shade of brown, with veins and veinlets still visible. Yet another is a humus-coloured patty whose label, written at the turn of the twentieth century, tells us that it contains remains of bald cypress and sequoia trees. These samples look and feel like vegetation. They are haptic reminders that what we call 'brown coal' is not the uniform and standardised material we know in the form of briquettes, but instead comprises the diagenetically transformed remains of photosynthetic beings which once made and remade these landscapes too.

Throughout the twentieth century, Bitterfeld's mining and manufacturing industries dug, dumped, mixed and churned the material legacies of these once active lifeworlds, discharging their material traces on a planetary scale. 'Bitterfeld is in everything' is a phrase we frequently heard from the city's long-time residents. I became particularly interested in a collection of photographs documenting some of the industrial processes in action around Bitterfeld. The gestures captured in motion are crude, violent and messy. In these photos lignite, groundwater, sugar beet and alkali cellulose, each having undergone various processes of transformation, are shown scattered through the air and water and on the ground, covering hands, clothes, hair and bodies. Yet the leaching of these materials is incommensurable with the predominant modernist narrative of extraction, that of the master, control and containment of homogenous and inert materials, which exist outside of history and without geography. A topographic map dating from 1987 that depicts the mined-out landscape as a 'blank space' propagates this narrative. What was once an inhabited place has become *Terra nullius;* it has quite literally disappeared. And yet, in spite of this, outside of modernist knowledge frameworks and concerns, Bitterfeld's earth continues to churn.

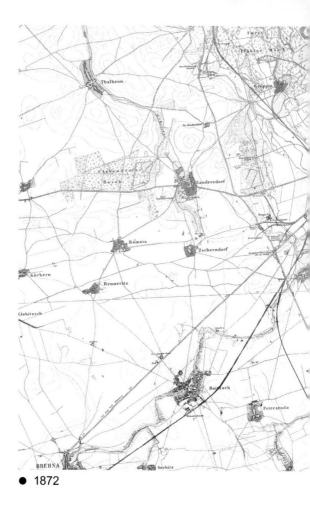

● 1872

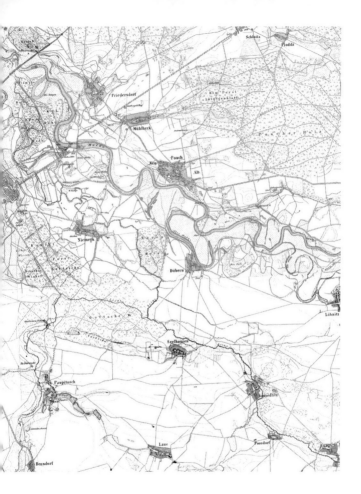

● 1987

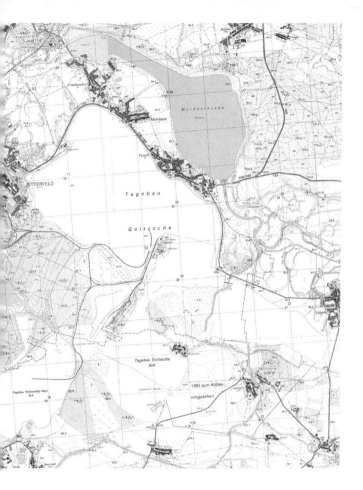

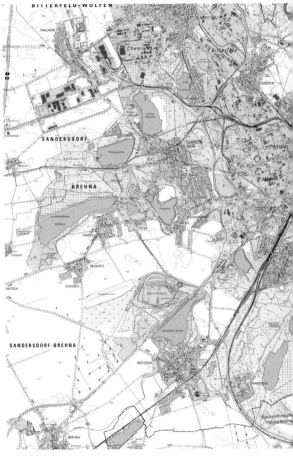

● 2021

Dr. Fred Walkow, the former head of Bitterfeld's environment agency and a former chemical engineer at the Agfa-Orwo Film Factory, showed me a series of photographs he took around Bitterfeld in the early 1990s. They are photographs of the ground which also show chemical transformations in action: iron oxidising out of a solution in an algae-rich and ferrous-red stream, burning phosphorus in a field of grass, ion exchangers in the form of pellets scattered across a contaminated riverbed. Seen as chemistry, these are active and vibrant landscapes in which chemical-industrial refuse and more-than-human metabolisms continue to remake the material substrates of the earth.

● Brown coal sample containing remains of bald cypress and sequoia trees. It was possibly found in Paupeitzsch, precise location unknown.

A hydrological map of Bitterfeld dated 2018 is scattered with small red, orange, yellow, pink and green dots, each one marking the site of a monitoring well made to gauge the chemical makeup of the groundwater. The wells are designed to detect and measure a handful of organic chemicals that are harmful to human life: BTEX, LHKW, vinyl chloride, chlorobenzene, monochlorobenzene and HCH. Lignite mining radically upset a carefully layered and stable stratigraphy that once held the region's two aquifers. No longer contained by impermeable geological layers, the groundwater leaches where it can towards bodies of surface water, into topsoil and into Bitterfeld's basements. Aiding a multi-channel transformation of its environment, it takes on a material load of mineral, chemical and metabolic byproducts whose interactions span timeframes ranging from nanoseconds to centuries.

The municipality of Bitterfeld is working continually to monitor and contain this aquiferous bubble as a matter of public utility. However, exactly what is being taken care of (other than the chemicals listed above) is not known by the chemists, the geologists or any of the institutionalised knowledge systems tasked with tending to the ground. Perhaps those best placed to attend to what is going on are the gardeners and the foresters, those in touch with the vegetation whose roots and branches reach out to detect and reciprocate with their subterranean environments. Whether appearing as a pine plantation or an overgrown back yard, entirely new ecosystems are coming into being from and within these filled and levelled grounds.

Lili Carr

Page seven of the influential biologist Raoul H. Francé's book *Lebender Braunkohlenwald* (Living Lignite Forest, 1932) illustrates the oil-based byproducts derived from coal mining in Bitterfeld.[1] The visual representation in the form of a tree not only situates coal at the centre, forming the life force of this region, but it also points to the abundance of industrially manufactured products derived from this plant-based fuel. The diagram may also be interpreted to provoke the idea that these chemical byproducts seep back into the soil within a natural biocycle. The contamination that remains hidden to the naked eye proliferates in the soil, alters the growth of vegetation and enters the food chain.

In order to bring forth a narrative through an architectural lens, my research situated the practices of everyday life and the mundane in the extraordinary context of the region; a landscape that due to chemical and coal production flourished economically but was environmentally destroyed. Focusing on the intimate domestic space of the home, kitchens became the representative microcosm of the Bitterfeld landscape, a space where coal could be traced in all its material forms and temporalities. Briquettes provided fuel for cooking. Plastics translated into amenities for modern kitchens that were manufactured by coal-powered industries.[2] But contamination also entered the home-cooked meal through polluted soil and vegetation. This creates a cyclic representation of the larger environmental and urban condition.

● Diagram showing oil-based byproducts derived from coal featured in Francés *Lebender Braunkohlenwald.*

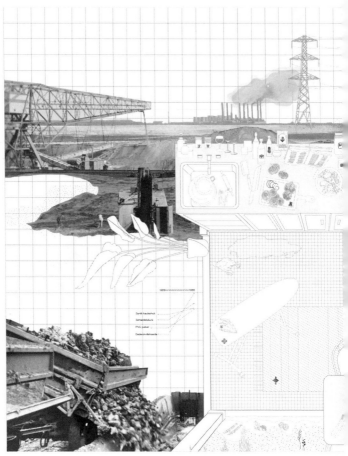

● *Coal Intimacies* by Shaiwanti Gupta, 2021. Illustration mapping the kitchen products derived from the coal and chemical industries.

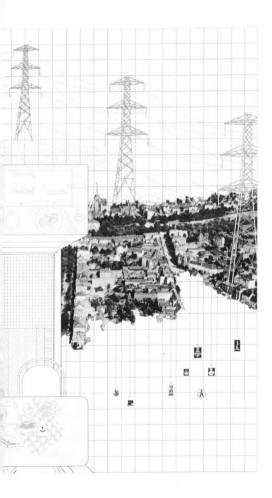

● Kindergarten teacher playing with children at the Agfa
Film Factory, 1958. During the GDR Agfa employed the
largest amount of female workers, a total of 8500, hence
they created space for childcare and hired caretakers for
500 infants.

The development of industries highly influenced the spatial
configuration and functional relevance of kitchens in the household. Around six thousand products that were manufactured in
Bitterfeld either directly or indirectly helped to mechanise the
modern kitchen. Kitchens became more compact and efficient,
expediting the cooking process.[3] With this mechanisation

process, women were given the opportunity to take on roles beyond the household. The industries in the GDR also empowered women by providing employment in large numbers. In addition to handling the delicate work of coating gelatin emulsion at the Agfa Film Factory, women were employed in labour intensive and technical jobs in power plants such as Kraftwerk Zschornewitz. Women played an active role in bringing food to the table quite literally.

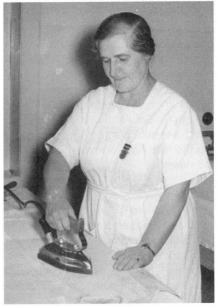

● Woman at work at the Agfa Film Factory, 1958.

Though the modernisation of the kitchen spread rapidly in post-war Germany, society was (re)constructed differently in the East and West. The design philosophy, aesthetic and material choices became political standpoints.[4] Evident in the magazines and cookbooks of the time, the role of women at home and the nature of repetitive labour[5] also took contradictory positions. Free time generated through appliances and electric stoves was encouraged to be utilised differently. While the Western consumer was indulged in the grooming of an ideal housewife, the Eastern consumer steered towards a work-life balance.[6] The Western objectification of cooking, and thereby women, can be seen in the popularity of cookbooks such as Lilo Aureden's *Was Männern so gut schmeckt* (What Men Like to Eat). However, cookbooks produced in the GDR position cooking as a parallel disposition in the life of working women. One such cookbook archived in the Kreismuseum Bitterfeld, *Kochen,* begins with the quote 'Eat so that your ears wiggle, work so that the heart leaps!'[7] This quote reflects the care placed in defining the recipes to suit the dietary needs of a hard-working individual.

Dismantling the space of the kitchen not only brings forth the ideas of domestic care, but also advocates for the systems of care at a societal level. Various formal and informal support structures were created to balance the complex matrix of labour division. Mutual aid was provided in the form of kindergartens, work canteens and laundry rooms, often run and financed by the employing industries, thus enabling the women to work.

Despite these efforts, the fact still remained that the lives of the people were tainted by the stunted growth of plants. Agricultural lands were made redundant, and crop produce became fatal due to absorbed toxicity. Oral narratives gathered from the residents in and around Bitterfeld highlight how homegrown tomatoes and lettuce were bought back from the residents to conceal the toxic condition of the soil, and it is still unfit for planting today.

Through the lens of the kitchen, we are able to see how to live and thrive in this region meant being engulfed in a toxic landscape. Everyday life and the ordinary were rooted in the extraordinary economics of toxicity. Home here is not seen as a closed system but as one that is connected with the inner and outer ecologies. The particularity of the region shaped the domestic practices of care while also shaping the individual, the progressive female and their innate relationship with this irredeemable landscape.

Shaiwanti Gupta

1 Francé, Raoul H., *Lebender Braunkohlenwald: Eine Reise durch die heutige Urwelt*, Stuttgart: Frankh, 1932.

2 Boehme, Katja (ed.), *Alles aus Plaste: Versprechen und Gebrauch in der DDR*, Cologne: Böhlau, 2012.

3 Meyer-Haagen, Elisabeth, *Das Elektrische Kochen*, Berlin Halensee: Linde, 1963.

4 Romijn, Peter, Scott-Smith, Giles, Segal, Joes, *Divided Dreamworlds? The Cultural Cold War in East and West*, Amsterdam: Amsterdam University Press, 2012, 155.

5 Federici, Silvia, *Revolution at Point Zero: Housework, Reproduction, and Feminist Struggle,* Oakland: PM Press, 2012.

6 Weinreb, Alice A., 'Matters of Taste: The Politics of Food and Hunger in Divided Germany 1945–1971', PhD Diss., Ann Arbor: University of Michigan Press, 2009.

7 Florstedt, Renate, *Kochen,* Leipzig: Verlag für die Frau, 1979.

Heat!

Architectural modernism is fundamentally environmental, but its environmentalism is ill-suited to address the current crises of planetary ecology. The origins of those crises are found in the entanglement of colonialism and capitalism over the past four centuries. This has wrought such havoc on our planet that the complicity of modern design is beyond question. After all, architects, designers, urban planners and engineers have provided some of the blueprints for how new modes of dispossession, extraction, fabrication, transportation and consumption were implemented. Decolonial activists and scholars have shown us how dominant orders of power and knowledge are rooted in the coloniality of an unequally shared global modernity. What if the very conviction that we can design our way out of an ecological crisis is equally bound to colonial ways of inhabiting the earth?

Modern architecture has not only been a terrain of experimentation with artificial constructions of the human environment; it has also been a field for their conceptualisation. When humans are normatively conceived as organisms immersed in environments that can be precisely qualified or quantified, their behaviour may be predicted and potentially transformed by altering those environments. Modernist ambitions to govern by design are thus based on a way of thinking that weaponises environmental determinism for the purposes of environmental determination. To address the current crises of planetary ecology, we need a theory and practice of design that instead fosters environmental autonomy. As Arturo Escobar has powerfully argued in

Designs for the Pluriverse, such design entails collaborative and place-based approaches that start from the 'radical interdependence of all beings'.

Kenny Cupers [1]

1 Guest speaker at the Bauhaus Lab 2021 International Symposium, 9 December 2021. Kenny Cupers is a Professor of Architectural History and Urban Studies at the University of Basel working at the intersection of architectural history, urban studies and critical geography. His research focuses on the role of housing in urban and state transformation, the epistemology and geopolitics of modernism, and the power and aesthetics of infrastructure.

'Instead of being yet another explanation of what we have lost, it is an exploration of what we might find [in landscapes].'
Simon Schama, 1995[1]

To step into the basement of the Bauhaus Dessau in the 1920s would have meant walking into a room filled with the approximately fifteen tons of raw coal and briquettes that were required to heat the entire building.[2] In this space today are the building's sanitary facilities and a cloakroom for visitors to leave their belongings. However, at floor level, on one of the building's facades you will see, through the windows, certain remnants of the former heating system. To become aware of the heating infrastructures of this building and its transitions entails coming to terms with the apparent contradictions of modernist cleanliness and its entanglements with ecological impacts and contamination. Reviewing the sociocultural and political history of the coal industry of the region led me on an entirely different research path towards a parallel history of nature conservation and stewardship as well as citizen-led initiatives of care.

How does revealing modernism's 'dirty' underbelly prompt reflections on what environmental thinking in this region looks like today? And how can this in turn affect the ways we conceive notions of infrastructure? These questions became a driving force of our collective research, which took on the form of a system, an infrastructure that considered analysing Hans Weber's herbarium[3] as an object, its effects and origins, in order to draw lines into the knowledge that exists beneath its surface. In addition, it was the speculative thought of this herbarium making an early claim on environmentalism in relation to air pollution that guided me to unearth the archive of the Kreismuseum Bitterfeld and examine it under the lens of shifting perceptions of nature.

● Exercise for the exhibition *Spur der Kohlen* by Bauhaus Dessau student Oliver Blomeier, 9–19 July 1993.

The museum's archive includes an extensive collection of photographs, newspaper clippings, archaeological findings, herbaria, domestic objects, paintings and more that represent the multiple layers present in this locality and its ever-changing landscape. It is as if the basement of this place encapsulates the fluctuating definitions and perceptions of nature and essentially conveys how, in Germany, environmental ideas have come to influence individuals across the political spectrum, from nationalist conservatives to socialists and green idealists.

● Items of the Kreismuseum Bitterfeld archive.

The contradictions and fluctuations became apparent through three particular findings. The first, a newspaper clipping dating back to 1925 whose headline addresses the success of a local settlement policy which stipulates that every green area in the city was to be protected by law against destruction. It also described the importance of protecting the city's natural spaces as recreational areas essential for the health of workers. Secondly, a folder that contained a series of posters which I would then learn were a part of a new kind of public outreach nature conservation programme *(Naturschutzwochen)* that began in 1957. The concept was tested in pilot projects conducted in Potsdam and Karl-Marx-Stadt and was later established throughout the GDR together with a woodland conservation programme *(Woche des Waldes)*. Each of the week-long programmes was dedicated to a centrally assigned conservation theme. Thirdly, a document dating from 1968 which contained an extract of Article 15 of the constitution of the GDR that lists soil as the most precious resource of Germany and states that nature must be protected for the wellbeing of its citizens.

These documents reveal how Germany's early twentieth century nature conservation *(Naturschutz)* and homeland protection *(Heimatschutz)* movements envisioned the ideal environment as an anthropogenic terrain that blended the natural, cultivated and built environments in an aesthetically harmonious whole.[4] However, the toxic legacies present in the Bitterfeld narrative completely subjugate the idea that industrialisation or progress, i.e., the built environment, can aesthetically and harmoniously coexist with the natural whole.

Yet they do very much make apparent just how interrelated politics, infrastructure and nature can be and how society in turn reacts to these tensions. Alongside this archival research we were also given the opportunity to meet and speak with three different actors working for nature protection in Bitterfeld at different points in time:

'There also existed an adaptation to pollution itself, not just to the fight against pollution. Meaning that part of the population had come to terms and also benefitted from it [industrialisation and its job opportunities] and did not see environmental pollution as a bad thing. For many people, environmental protection became the enemy.' Fred Walkow [5]

'Libraries were also very strongly regulated in GDR times. They had the task of collecting and imparting knowledge to others, but our approach was also to use this passing-on of knowledge to get people to take action. We wanted to bring people together and get them to act. And maybe that was our good fortune, to be able to do something completely new.' Heidi Karstedt [6]

'In my generation, the biggest problem is that people can see the problems but don't want to take action, to do anything about them. [...] My generation expects solidarity.' Jonas Venediger [7]

● A selection of the *Naturschutzwochen* posters from the Kreismuseum Bitterfeld archive presented in the exhibition *Vegetation under Power.*

Juxtaposing these testimonies with the archival findings points to how infrastructure is more than physical material; its sources and aftermaths have rippling effects. But what I propose is to view Bitterfeld not as a history of extractivism but more as a history of stewardships that has been interrupted by extractivism. Landscapes can also express the virtues of a social community.

Maya Errázuriz

1   As cited in: De Soto, Hermione G., 'Contested Landscapes. Reconstructing Environment and Memory in Postsocialist Saxony-Anhalt', in Berdahl, Daphne, Bunzl, Matti, Lampland, Martha (eds.), *Altering States: Ethnographies of Transition in Eastern Europe and the Former Soviet Union,* Ann Arbor: The University of Michigan Press, 2000, 103.

2   Markgraf, Monika, *Archaeology of Modernism. Preservation of the Bauhaus Dessau,* Berlin: Jovis, 2021.

3   The point of departure of the Bauhaus Lab 2021: a collection of leaves recollected during 1931 in the Goitzsche area in Bitterfeld now archived in the Kreismuseum Bitterfeld. For further context refer to pages 9 and 10.

4   Lekan, Thomas, Zeller, Thomas, *Germany's Nature: Cultural Landscapes and Environmental History,* New Brunswick: Ruttgers University Press, 2005, 3.

5   Head of Bitterfeld's environment agency from 1991 to 2015.

6   Founder and librarian of Bitterfeld's Umweltbibliothek from 1991 to the late-1990s/early 2000s.

7   18-year-old Fridays for Future Bitterfeld activist, 2021.

● Hot air balloon advertises Bitterfeld's Umwelt-bibliothek. Image featured in the *Bitterfelder Zeitung*, August 1993.

A photograph retrieved from the Kreismuseum Bitterfeld archive captures the laying of a broad-gauge rail line overseen and worked on by Soviet soldiers wearing their M73 uniforms with traditional pilotka hats. Bearing the inscription *'Bitterfeld 1977, Sowjetische Soldaten helfen beim Verlegen von Gleisen in einem Braunkohletagebau'* (Bitterfeld 1977, Soviet soldiers help lay tracks in a lignite open cast mine), the image is a compelling piece of evidence that attests to the complex history of industrialisation in the GDR but gives little indication of the corresponding environmental effects. Indeed, one could postulate that the image is just that—an 'official' document. Its high exposure, black-and-white character betrays little information apart from the work undertaken by the soldiers, working in a would-be sterile, lunar landscape; an 'official' document that owing to its placelessness could provide little ammunition to the growing discontentment with the environmental conditions in the region.

If mining lignite, better known as brown coal, had driven manufacturing and metallurgical industries in the region known as Saxony since the 1840s, in the Weimar Republic it drove infrastructural development in the form of electrical power grids to and from Berlin. Post 1945 the region underwent significant environmental and geopolitical restructuring beginning with the establishment of COMECON (the Council for Mutual Economic Assistance), the 'Eastern' response to the Marshall Plan, in 1949. The trade partnership necessitated a significant expansion of heavy industry in the GDR to accommodate imports and the processing of raw materials as well as the export of finished goods, tools and machinery.

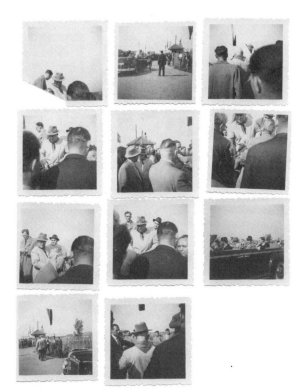

● Images of Comrade Nikita Khrushchev's visit to Bitterfeld during the 5th congress of the SED, the ruling party of the GDR. This visit was followed by the 1959 Bitterfelder Konferenz (Bitterfeld conference) held at the Kulturpalast Bitterfeld, which was the starting point of the *Bitterfelder Weg,* an initiative encouraging workers to be writers too.

● Soviet soldiers laying tracks in a lignite opencast mine, Bitterfeld 1977.

Initially, this conduit for the payment of reparations visually cemented the Soviet influence and presence in the GDR. But in 1953, a series of coordinated local uprisings against the ruling party, the SED and the *Sowjetische Aktiengesellschaft* (SAG or Soviet joint-stock companies) resulted in the rapid repression of uprisings and, to some degree, a smaller militaristic presence.[1] So why is it that, twenty years later, this photograph wilfully disregards the question of the environment and simultaneously aggrandises the presence of Soviet troops and the building of coal transport infrastructure in the region?

The answer lies partly in the ways in which infrastructural development was once again a key feature of East Germany's post-war reconstruction plans. Against the backdrop of the Non-Aligned Conference of 1961, socialist countries were increasingly drawn together in a tightly woven web of diplomatic machinations and construction projects. These ranged from the Druzhba (friendship) oil pipeline constructed in 1964 that connected Siberia with the GDR, Poland, Belarus, Ukraine, Austria and Czechoslovakia to smaller rail connections as pictured in the photograph.

Environmental pollution was not coincidental to these socialist ties and declarations of friendship beyond the 1953 incidents. While the question of nature has long been debated in Marxist discourse, as many historians have noted, the instrumentalisation of nature was a state-led project that teetered on the socialist-capitalist divide.[2] Indeed, if brown coal in the GDR was a significant energy resource and a bulwark against Soviet politics, it also provided jobs for its citizens, which nonetheless had significant ecological costs in the form of dispossessed agricultural lands, brownfields, groundwater depletion, and air/water pollution. These severely dented the image of the GDR's policy towards a balance of 'economy and ecology'.[3]

During the 1973 energy crisis, reduced access to oil reserves in the USSR meant that the GDR increased its reliance on domestic brown coal as a primary energy source, reversing to some extent the dependence on imported oil. By some accounts, by 1985, 85 per cent of electricity consumption relied on the burning of coal.[4] This renewed centrality of coal to everyday life is perhaps best captured by returning to the archive of the Kreismuseum Bitterfeld and its records of the exhibition *Die Entstehung der Kohle* in 1977.[5] But the intention of the photograph, taken in the same year, is different from a mere embrace of coal and yields a different story from the grandiose infrastructural developments in the region: one of the repression of, and dissent by, environmental groups that sought to highlight the scale of the environmental damage.

Curiously, 'green dissident' activities mirrored the spaces of transnational networks of infrastructural development.[6] Emboldened by the release of reports on issues such as transboundary air pollution by the Geneva Convention, oppositional groups found solidarity in resuscitating environmental concerns through underground and covert networks of information dissemination. By the 1980s, environmental issues were no longer only about flora and fauna but extended to include peace, demilitarisation, democratisation, *glasnost* and *perestroika* as well as solidarity with the developing world.[7]

In recognising this confluence of themes taken up by opposition groups, the photograph offers one more reading of the complex history of coal in the region. This veers away from a moral argument of environmental destruction to allow for readings of coal extraction that were in some way foundational for new kinds of imagined communities in the Socialist Bloc. Here, if only in the metaphorical sense, the railway lines appear to be the precise piece that connected the brown coal fields of Bitterfeld with dissident activities across the border and at home.

Shivani Shedde

1 Geerling, Wayne, Magee, Gary B., Smyth, Russell, 'Occupation, Reparations, and Rebellion: The Soviets and the East German Uprising of 1953', *Journal of Interdisciplinary History* 52, no. 2, MIT Press, Autumn 2021: 225–250; Vale, Michel, Bethkenhagen, Jochen, 'The Development of GDR Economic Relations with the USSR', *International Journal of Politics* 12, no. 1/2, Spring-Summer, 1982, GDR Foreign Policy Part II: 232–260.
2 For a comprehensive bibliography on the question of ecology and Marxism, see Andreas Malm's web essay, https://www.historicalmaterialism.org/reading-guides/ecology-marxism-andreas-malm. For a discussion on the GDR and questions of the environment see: Rubin, Eli, 'The Greens, the Left and the GDR: A Critical Reassessment', in Mödersheim, Sabine, Moranda, Scott, Rubin, Eli (eds.), *Ecologies of Socialisms: Germany, Nature and the Left in History, Politics, and Culture*, Berlin: Peter Lang, 2019, 167–199.

3 Quoted in: Ault, Julia, *Saving Nature Under Socialism: Trans-national Environmentalism in East Germany, 1968–1990, Cambridge: Cambridge University Press,* 129. Various state-led education programmes to educate the public about the costs of environmental destruction have been discussed in the previous essay by Maya Errázuriz.

4 DeBardeleben, Joan, 'The Future Has Already Begun. Environmental Damage and Protection in the GDR', *International Journal of Sociology* 18, no. 4, winter 1988–1989: 144–164, 145.

5 Translation: The origin of coal.

6 Jordan, Carlo, 'Greenway – das Osteuropäische Grüne Netzwerk 1985–1990', in Heinrich Böll Stiftung (ed.), Grünes Gedächtnis 2010. See also accounts of the Polish trade union Solidarność.

7 Becker, C. (1990). Umweltgruppen in der DDR. In: DDR-Jugend. VS Verlag für Sozialwissenschaften. https://doi.org/10.1007/978-3-322-93750-6_9

Breath!

HOW DOES ONE 'LIVE WITH' TOXICITY?

Making sense of the Bitterfeld Kulturpalast after reunification accentuates a deep ideological divide and a haunting industrial legacy of a once-divided Germany. Due to the building's unfavourable location at a high point of the water table, it has been forced to endure the steady pressure of contaminated groundwater on its foundation since its construction in the 1950s. After more than one and a half centuries of excessive brown coal extraction and chemical production in the region, the groundwater is saturated with chemicals that have caused substantial damage to the building's substance and necessitated its closure to the public in 2010. Closing the building has moreover left a haunting void in the community's socio-cultural, spiritual fabric, as the people no longer have a place to meet en masse. But despite astronomical federal spending on remedial efforts to pump and treat the groundwater in the region over the last 30 years, it was recently publicly acknowledged that it is doomed to do so indefinitely. Bitterfeld will always need to live with its toxicity.

The relation between brown coal and chemicals and the community they contributed to forming is thus co-constitutive. Just as the communal activities that used to fill the interiors of the Kulturpalast with life lie archived in the memories of the community, so too has the toxic exposure ingrained itself in their DNA and that of their offspring. Life and its continuity in the region will forever be tightly intertwined with the chemicals and the coal that gave birth to them, forging profound relations that span generations and geography. Just as the Kulturpalast's material presence is linked with all the lives that gave it vitality and meaning, it will be forever plagued by the chronically contaminated groundwater that will always co-exist with it. To live with toxicity is simply a condition of life, and there is a need to find ways of learning to live with its permanence and pay careful attention to all its loose ends.

Caroline Ektander[1]

1 Guest speaker at the Bauhaus Lab 2021 International Symposium, 9 December 2021. Caroline Ektander is an architect, writer and independent researcher with an un-relenting interest in understanding and engaging with waste practices and politics in a time of ecological crisis. She is also one of the founders of Toxic Commons, a platform that acts on toxic dissemination and the environmental injustices inherent to it.

My contribution to the exhibition was a short film in which Hans Weber's herbarium is documented and mediated through the roaming gaze of an electron microscope. It was an attempt to reveal the unseen or unrepresentable traces that were speculated to live in the herbarium specimens. The microscopic image alluded to the changing epistemes of visuality, objectivity and representation in the scientific imaginary of the early twentieth century. In addition to the Weber herbarium, there are intercuts of brown coal imaged from various perspectives.

It is this connection–the metabolic link between sunlight, vegetal life, energy flows, photosynthesis–that led me towards photographic practices. I was drawn to the histories of the former site of the Agfa-Orwo Film Factory in Bitterfeld-Wolfen. To me, this place lives on the threshold between the afterlife of film production and image-based practices, where the oculocentric paradigms that organise the world around the human eye become murky. It was a site that asked of us to think about contamination and exposure, about labour performed in darkness and about the vibrant ecologies that underlie film production.[1]

In her essay 'Photosynthetic mattering: Rooting into the Planthroposcene', Natasha Myers invites us to think about the creatures whose metabolisms rearrange matter and energy and worldly scales. This is a provocative image of enormous biochemical forces that are the product of life and death, distributing and rearranging elements, minerals and energy. 'Plants', Natasha writes, 'are the substance,

● Plant fossils were common byproducts of the coal mining industry, imprints of the cyclical metabolisms of the earth. Photo from the Deutsches Bergbau-Museum Bochum, 2021.

substrate, scaffolding, symbol, sign and sustenance of political economies the world over. What are fossil fuels and plastics but the petrified bodies of once-living photosynthetic creatures? We have thrived and we will die, burning their energetic accretions. And so it is not an overstatement to say that we are only because they are.'[2]

Alongside my colleagues, my time in Bitterfeld was spent thinking through strata.[3] This meant addressing temporalities that far exceeded the timelines of photographic histories,

● The kaleidoscopic surface of a brown coal briquette as seen through an electron microscope. Still from the short film *Herbarium,* 2021.

and recognising that the human visual apparatus also carries an environmental weight. This is in many ways a response to the ubiquitous place of images in a culture of exhausting hypervisibility and the recognition that photography is still very much a link to archive, evidence and memory.[4]

Like many other practitioners that work with images, I think a lot about their afterlife. The future of images can take on many forms, whether they spring from computational realms, through modelling, GANs or data. One thing that remains constant, however, is that the gaze of new imaging technologies still turns towards the natural world, tracking it and abstracting it, making it legible for later consumption.[5] This gaze zooms its carbon-intensive oculus through scales which were once unimaginable.

One of the main themes of our research involved thinking about infrastructures and their energetic metabolisms, how they powered and sustained the photochemical combine in Bitterfeld.[6] Energy infrastructures are thus encoded into the very materiality of film, undeniably sustained by fossil capitalism and its energetic flows. To this day, even in the most abstract computational spaces, images are networked to the carbon metabolisms of the earth.

Every molecule of silver in a photographic film can be traced to hundreds of billions of years ago when precious metals were formed during extreme stellar events. As if probing into geological and mineral layers of the earth, light oxidises and burns the silver with its inscriptions.

● Machinery producing film at the Agfa-Orwo Film Factory (now the Industrie- und Filmmuseum Wolfen).

The milky gelatin membrane of photographic emulsion formed from the ashes of cattle bone holds collective memories suspended in animal life through an array of microscopic grains.[7]

It is this photographic stratigraphy that I wished to penetrate in my approach to this project to see behind the epidermal layer of images and to dig into the chemical ecologies behind their production. This drew me to begin a series of experiments with photographic processes and chemistry to rethink the materials that are left behind in the darkroom.

In darkroom photography, there are processing rituals that use corrosive, polluting and sensitising chemistry in order to produce images. Yet, before film even makes its way into the darkroom, it undergoes many transformations that take place under darkness. The extraction of coal, lignite, silver, gold is labour that is often performed in the dark. We heard anecdotes about the workers in the Film Factory, particularly women, who laboured in darkness for hours on end. The human eye, sophisticated as it may be, is still an adaptation to living above ground.

To me, the darkroom has always been a place of intimacy and touch. Human skin inevitably has a close encounter with photographic chemistry as it makes contact with the porous membrane that is our skin. This is something I learned the hard way as a young photographer who developed skin sensitivities due to exposure to darkroom chemistry. This amphibian barrier that provides our bodies with a certain level of protection is nonetheless not as individuated as we think.[8]

In the darkroom, we breathe in and exhale the scent of developer and fixer, an exchange happens between our breath and the sublimating fumes.

Historically, exposures, contaminations and chemical frictions reconfigured the social and ecological relations in communities around Bitterfeld-Wolfen. A shift occurred towards relations of enclosure, in which the maintenance of containment infrastructures becomes a public utility. The ongoing work of remediation reveals that despite valiant efforts, a techno-fix is often not enough. Rather, the work of transformation means reconsidering the lifespans of chemical species and the possibilities of life after pollution.[9]

Fixing was the mechanism that allowed photography to flourish. Fugitive images ceased to fade and instead became permanently inscribed onto a surface, pausing the oxidation of the silver halides on a photographic membrane. This paradigmatic relationship to images and fixing is sustained by fossil fuels, chemical leakages and contamination. The cost of memory is precariously rooted in the ecologies and communities that together breathe the legacy of the Agfa-Orwo Film Factory.

Nancy Dayanne Valladares

● Photographic experiment: A solution of sodium hypochlorite dissolves the layers of photographic emulsion on black-and-white sheet film.

1 Jane Bennet's notion of vibrancy has been a crucial tool to rethink photochemical agencies.

2 Myers, Natasha, 'Photosynthetic Mattering: Rooting into the Planthroposcene', in Thorsen, Line Marie (ed.) *Moving Plants,* Rønnebæksholm: Narayana Press, 2017, 123–129.

3 Thanks to Shivani Shedde for the insightful conversations on stratigraphy and sedimentation.

4 Dewdney, Andrew, *Forget Photography,* 1st ed., London: Goldsmiths University Press, 2021.

5 Many thanks to Elisabetta Rattalino for her insights into botanising, naturalist histories and vegetal connections.

6 Shaiwanti Gupta's work on networks of heat in the home are closely linked to these metabolisms.

7 I credit these connections with silver to conversations with Boaz Levin, whose ongoing research into the histories of the Film Factory opened up possibilities for returning photography.

8 Mendes, Margarida, Admiss, Danielle-Maria, Shotwell, Alexis, 'The Body is Not a Sovereign Object', Transmediale Podcast, 2021, https://transmediale.de/almanac/the-body-is-not-a-sovereign-object.

9 Shapiro, Nicolas, Kirksey, Eben, Chemo-Ethnography: An Introduction', *Cultural Anthropology* 32, no. 4, 481 -493, https://journal.culanth.org/index.php/ca/article/view/ca32.4.01/182.

Lignite, also known as brown coal, is soft and woody in texture. Leftover plant matter from peat can sometimes still be distinguished within its coarse structure. With a high moisture content and a low heating value, it is considered a low-grade coal. The formation of the lignite deposits found in the Bitterfeld area can be dated back to the Paleocene, sixty-six to fifty-six million years ago. Once, the landscape of this region was composed of swamps and marshland; the name Bitterfeld means 'boggy land'. Through the application of heat, pressure and, most importantly, time, concentrated plant material in these ancient habitats was compressed under rocky sedimentation layers to chemically and physically transform it into a combustible and carbon-rich rock.

The geological timeline of lignite formation is considered recent when compared to that of black or bituminous coals. The brown coal seam can therefore be found under as little as ten to twenty metres of overburden, allowing for the extraction technique of open-pit mining. In the map of the company VEB Braunkohlenwerk Welzow, the open cast mines of the region of Central Germany are represented by blue and pink zones. The red lines show the railway system that carried the brown coal to power stations where it would be burned for fuel.

During the Bauhaus Lab 2021, we had the opportunity to meet people who had worked with brown coal in the GDR. Everyone was closely tied to this resource because coal had been an economic and social foundation for many communities. It provided fuel for power plants that created electricity,

● VEB Braunkohlenwerk map of open-cast mines and railway systems outlined on a map of Saxony-Anhalt, 1987.

celluloid for the film industry, briquettes to heat houses and clay to build houses, found in the overburden. However, the enormous scale of open-cast mines would also mean the displacement of 120 communities[1] in the region of Central Germany, relocating over 40,000 people. Maps continuously changed as towns and villages disappeared.

● The Golpa-Nord open-cast mine.

We interviewed a man named Roland Hermann who grew up in Gremmin, a municipality three kilometres northwest of Graefenhainichen. His family had lived there for generations, back when the landscape was forests and grasses and the main economic activity came from agriculture. In 1982, Gremmin was demolished to make way for the Golpa-Nord open-cast mine although the actual relocation for its inhabitants came years ahead of this date. For our interview, he asked to meet at the former site of Golpa-Nord, which today has been converted into an open-air museum known as Ferropolis. The lake that surrounds the museum is called Gremminer See, an homage to the village of Gremmin that used to stand there.

From our conversation, it is clear that coal leaves a complicated legacy. As relocated citizens lost all physical remnants of their homes, resettlement sometimes provided an opportunity for younger people to move into their own places and access more modernised buildings and amenities. The coal industry provided security through its jobs and infrastructures, and it shaped a general way of life in the GDR. Even as it transformed and polluted the natural environment, the resource of coal must have also felt infinite and therefore reassuring.

1   Ess, Julia, 'Re-Location: Urban and architectural analysis of resettlement practices in the brown coal mining area of Welzow-Süd in East Germany', SHS Web of Conferences 63, 13002, 2019, https://doi.org/10.1051/shsconf/20196313002.

Extract from our interview with Roland Hermann:

Many places had to give way to coal during this period. How did you receive the news that Gremmin would be resettled?

The pit itself had actually been announced years earlier because the surveys had already been made in Gremmin in the 1930s. Coal had been discovered under the ground there. But it was only in the late 1950s that mining started here in Gremmin. In fact, a burial ban had already been issued in the cemetery. There was also a construction ban. Then in 1968 Gremmin stepped back from open-pit mining because it was said that the GDR would now get oil from Russia, the Soviet Union back then. Then we were told that the bodies could remain in the cemetery, there would be no further excavation, and people were allowed to be buried there again. We were even allowed to build. No new buildings, but we could do repair work. But in 1970 all that suddenly stopped. It was announced that Gremmin would be resettled. In meetings, they said, 'Everyone will be provided with an apartment.' We were relatively good citizens and didn't protest much. But for people like my father, who had to move when he was seventy years old, and others, who were even older, that was of course a very heavy blow. It was a bit chaotic too. But that was the case everywhere in the places that fell victim to lignite mining at the time, it was so common then.

Elizabeth Hong

Growth!

A herbarium, despite its endeavour to classify and perhaps systematise, is necessarily something fragmented and fragmenting, a forever unfulfilled wish to save, to preserve, for instance by drying leaves, flowers or entire plants. But on each one of its pages, regardless of a variety of specimens, it displays the same shape: the shape of death. What herbaria ultimately preserve is not only vulnerable and fragile; it is also, above all, fragility itself.

Fragments of the plant world are selected with great care and attention. But in so doing, they are cut off from the natural contexts (the times and the places) of their growth and displayed in a book where they are juxtaposed with their accidental neighbours. Herbaria are places of contact: of a leaf in an album with the leaf of a tree, of a gliding gaze and a vegetal shape, of the materials used to mount specimens, parts of plants and the page. It is through the surfaces and their intersections that herbaria communicate with their viewers as well as, somewhat mysteriously, with themselves. The surface-to-surface encounter creates an interface that is distinct from the thick milieu from which fragments of flowers have been culled. This interface is the time and place of the Hegelian spirit which, contrary to the intuitions of the past century, is not at all allergic to fragments or the processes of fragmentation.

Herbaria are silent howls, frozen, suspended in time and space, cut off from lived durations and habitats. They are products of Western science, which is itself a product of Western metaphysics with its dreams of freezing being itself, of putting the selfsame in immutable moulds that resist the tendencies of change, generation, decay and metamorphosis. It is these millennia-old dreams that turn out to be environmental nightmares when they are realized in the perverse shape of non-decomposable, non-biodegradable, 'stable' materials.

Nevertheless, herbaria also have an upside of accentuating everything that Western metaphysics considers dispensable: the surface, contact between surfaces, a visible form, colour, the physicality of appearance, which is something that goes against our usual obsession with depth and the devalorisation of surfaces. Could we imagine, perhaps, herbaria as the tools of immanent resistance to the metaphysical drive from which they originated?

Michael Marder[1]

1 Guest speaker at the Bauhaus Lab 2021 International Symposium, 9 December 2021. Michael Marder is an IKERBASQUE Research Professor in the department of philosophy at the University of the Basque Country (UPV/EHU), Vitoria-Gasteiz, Spain. His work spans the fields of phenomenology, environmental philosophy and political thought.

The Kreismuseum Bitterfeld holds a significant botanical collection. Crystallised in the taxonomic organisation provided
by Werner Rothmaler's *Exkursionsflora von Deutschland*
(1962) since the 1990s, the collection bears no apparent
testimony to the drastic environmental transformations the
district underwent in the twentieth century. Unlike more modern herbaria,[1] plant sheets do not describe the ecological
context of a plant extraction. By simply looking at a plant's
documentation and without knowing a species's ecology, we
might not be able to tell whether a specimen had been collected, for instance, in an ancient forest or alongside a lignite
mine. But suppose we conceive of herbaria not solely in terms
of their taxonomic drive but, more generally, as practices
that formalise situated human encounters with their sur-
rounding environment. In that case, we could rethink them
as complex social and cultural constellations that allow us
to root the collection in the shifting ecology of Bitterfeld and
its surroundings.

Cross-referencing the handwritten notes on the plant sheets
with the inventory of the museum's herbarium, we learned
that it was not a single-handed endeavour. It was a long-
term effort, begun by the founder of the museum, the local
historian Emil Obst, and continued in the 1930s by sever-
al museum associates. These included Wilhelm Fueß of
Dessau, who worked as a headmaster in Roitzsch, and the
chemist Dr. Ernst Hanschke. They were both also mem-
bers of a working group for the flora of Central Germany (Arbeitsgemeinschaft zur Erforschung der Pflanzen-
welt von Mitteldeutschland) led by Prof. Wilhelm Troll and

EXKURSIONSFLORA

VON DEUTSCHLAND

GEFÄSSPFLANZEN

Herausgegeben von Prof. Dr. Werner Rothmaler

Bearbeiter: Hans Förster, Papstdorf (Post Königstein) · Dr. Franz Fukarek, Greifswald
Willi Lemke, Jena · Erich Püschel, Berlin · Hellmuth Reichenbach, Rodewisch i. Vogtl.
Prof. Dr. Werner Rothmaler, Greifswald

Dritte, verbesserte Auflage
Mit 823 Abbildungen

▼
▼▼

VOLK UND WISSEN VOLKSEIGENER VERLAG BERLIN
1962

vorhanden im Herbar Bitterfeld:
x aus dem Kreisgebiet u. angrenzenden Gebiet
o woandersher
unbestimmtes nützliches Exemplar   z = zwei
1 ohne Fundort

● Frontispiece of Werner Rothmaler's *Exkursionsflora von Deutschland*, 1962, annotated by Ms. Einenkel.

Hermann Meusel at the University of Halle in the second half of the 1930s. During the GDR era, Ms. Einenkel, an employee of the Kreismuseum Bitterfeld, took care of inventorying, organising and expanding the collection. In these times, private citizens donated smaller herbaria to the museum. This was the case with the herbarium of the botanist Hans Weber that elicited our research at the Bauhaus Lab 2021, as well as the one assembled by the aspiring pharmacist Peter Feige in 1949.

Although all follow the Linnaean taxonomic model, each collector's plant sheets have their individual formal qualities. Not only does the backing paper change, but the textual information and the arrangement of plants also vary, possibly corresponding to different botanical cultures. In the collection, we can identify plant sheets where the scientific imperative is more evident. Einenkel's samples from the 1960s onwards resonate with more modern herbaria. They present a species using an individual specimen delicately taped to white paper and labelled with the name of the species, the location and date of its finding. After collecting samples in the Goitzsche area, Peter Feige instead glued each plant in its entirety (leaves, flowers and roots system) to a thick, light blue porous paper. Interestingly, each of his records documents not only the family and genus of the specimen but also its potential medical use. In this feature, we can acknowledge an affinity with the origins of herbaria as Renaissance *orti sicci* and the role that applied botany still played in the training of chemists. We could also suggest that earlier plant records, such as Emil Obst's, might have not been solely prompted by scientific inquiry.

● Peter Feige, herbarium sheet *(Galanthus nivalis)*, 1949.

Name, lat.: *Galanthus nivalis*
Name, dt.: *Schneeglöckchen*
Familie: *Amaryllidaceae*
Droge:
Bestandteile:

Verwendung:

Fundort: *Garten*

● Emil Obst, herbarium sheet (multiple species), ca. 1918.

Obst's plant sheets present compelling compositions of different specimens that are unconnected. On one page in a more extensive series, there are nine specimens of as many species: a snowdrop *(Galanthus nivalis)*, a cornflower *(Centaurea cyanus)*, a fumitory *(Fumaria officinalis)*, a tiny heather branch *(Calluna vulgaris)*, a forget-me-not *(Miosotis intermedia)*, wallflowers *(Cheiranthus cheiri)*, some dodder *(Cuscuta epithymum)* with its red tendrils intertwined with the branches of a conehead thyme plant *(Thymus capitus)*, and a lungwort *(Pulmonaria officinalis)*. Except for the lungwort and the forget-me-not *(Boraginaceae)*, they all belong to different taxonomic families. They are neither used for similar medical purposes – lungwort was traditionally used for chest pain relief whilst the fumitory was named after its ability to irritate the eye as with smoke – nor do they bloom in the same season. Snowdrops, for instance, sprout at the tail end of winter, cornflowers in the warmer months of the year. Let us also consider that Obst collected the flowering or leafy parts of the plants only. Although accompanied by their scientific name, it appears that their grouping eludes a scientific rationale and embraces an aesthetic one instead.

Obst possibly collected plants, and especially flowers, for their beauty. Botany as a hobby had become a fashionable entertainment for the wealthier social classes since Goethe's days.[2] Additionally, the study of plants had been a key element of applied art education since the late 1800s and the fashion for Art Nouveau, thus suggesting a taste for vegetal motives.[3] This trend continued over the following decades. Although with different aims and approaches, the study of plants was not irrelevant even at the Bauhaus. As a collector of natural *mirabilia* and plant fragments,[4] Paul Klee invited his students to observe and draw plants and their growth for the purpose of creating intrinsically dynamic forms, as reported in his teaching notebooks. In *The New Vision* (1928), we read that László Moholy-Nagy drew on the idea of plants as inventors and biotechnology as conceived by botanist Raoul H. Francé (1920).[5] At the Bauhaus, this approach did not exclude the possibility of appreciating the sheer beauty of flowers, as seen in the delicate photographs of Ruth Hollós-Consemüller.

● Woman collecting snow-drops in the Goitzsche, 1922, photographer unknown.

In the creation of Obst's herbarium, showing the aesthetic qualities of plants was not essential. In the 1923 pamphlet *Die Goitzsche bei Bitterfeld in der Literatur, und ihr Anspruch auf Naturdenkmals = Schutz,* Obst had supported the candidature of the Goitzsche floodplain, its flora and fauna, as a community natural monument. Thus, it is more likely that the herbarium he assembled intended to demonstrate the aesthetic and environmental worth of the area at a time when the native land was under siege from the expansion of local chemical industries and coal mining. The Goitzsche, Obst claimed, was intrinsically associated with the local identity and praised for its paradisiacal beauty by prominent travellers. The progressive destruction of the Goitzsche, its flora and fauna, was perceived as immensely damaging to the local landscape and the welfare of the community living locally. It thus appears that his plant collection developed from his affection for his homeland and the urgency for nature protection in the early days of environmental changes. The legacy of Obst's operation reverberates in the very presence of a botanical collection in the Kreismuseum Bitterfeld. Standing as an unprecedented attempt to salvage a land that no longer exists, it preserves a fragile and fragmented memory of an erased ecosystem.

Elisabetta Rattalino

● Ruth Hollós-Consemüller, untitled (Snowdrops), 1920/1929,
Bauhaus Dessau Foundation (I 44716).

1 Willis, Kathy, Fry, Carolyn, *Plants: From Roots to Riches,* London: John Murray Pubs, 2015, 31–43.
2 Koerner, Lisbet, 'Goethe's Botany: Lessons of a Feminine Science', *Isis,* vol. 84, no. 3, 1993, 470–495.
3 Thümmler, Sabine, 'The Botanization of Art', in Doll, Nikola, Bredekamp, Horst, Schäffner, Wolfgang (eds.), *+ultra knowledge & gestaltung,* Leipzig: E. A. Seemann Verlag, 2017, 89–94.
4 Grote, Ludwig (ed.), *Erinnerungen an Paul Klee,* Munich: Prestel, 1959, 73.
5 Moholy-Nagy, László. *The New Vision and Abstract of an Artist,* New York: Wittenborn/Schultz, 1947, 29.

Our collective research started by opening the folders of a herbarium of the flora collected around Bitterfeld in 1931 by Hans Weber. We approached this herbarium as a silent witness to the industrialisation of this region during the early twentieth century. Some traces of dust on a few plants possibly contain ashes from the power plants or various chemical industries in Bitterfeld. These 'damages', materialised as small stains or holes on dried leaves, teach us that herbaria contain more than plants. Opening, one by one, the folders of this herbarium in the Kreismuseum Bitterfeld created a certain kind of expectation about the invisible toxicity of these former industries. This experience guided the way I looked at the vegetation present in Bitterfeld and its surroundings over the course of three months.

In an attempt to investigate the postindustrial landscapes of Bitterfeld, practicing botany provided a spontaneous starting point to dive into this research. Collecting plants to create a herbarium involves being in the landscape, walking across fields and getting close to the ground. The specific time of a collection allows people to observe and think about the transformations of the land. In 1931, Hans Weber collected most of the plants in the herbarium from the Goitzsche forest. This forest was entirely felled at the end of the 1940s to dig a large-scale open-cast lignite mine which operated until 1991. To refill this gigantic mine, in the early 2000s the adjacent Mulde river was diverted into the hole to create an artificial lake of clean water. The Bitterfeld region is shaped by these successive disfigurements, induced by the needs and consequences of industrialisation. A lake that used to be a mine, which was once a forest.

● Hans Weber's herbarium, *Ulmus montana Withering*, 1931.

● Collecting leaves in Bitterfeld, 2021.

In 2021, while collecting leaves mostly around the Goitzsche lake – this research took place in autumn, between September and December – I realised that the biochemical reaction which is taking place in their surfaces is already a kind of infrastructure. Indeed, through photosynthesis, the leaves absorb carbon from the atmosphere and release the oxygen we breathe; the first relationship humans and plants have is this invisible exchange of substances happening through breathing. Plants create their environments, participate in the shape of the landscape and transform the airscape through the process that takes place in their leaves.[1] Some of the vegetation in Bitterfeld has been used for that purpose, to purify the air from smoke and particles.

Collecting leaves with anomalies and stains, and gathering them by location, was a way to engage in a dialogue with Hans Weber's herbarium, especially with Bitterfeld's vegetation and its surroundings, ninety years on. I speculated that some of these unusual spots may be a material and visible reaction to their environment, an exposure to contaminated land, water or air. Others may be the consequence of natural phenomena like the weather conditions or even the start of autumn.

Each leaf was photographed with a scanner quickly after picking it to record its original appearance, preserve it from decay and to zoom in on details as a microscope would do. Extracted from the original leaf, some anomalies became abstract colour changes or islands, open to speculation. This layout offers a close look at the surfaces of these common leaves and questions the potential of the herbarium as a visual medium. Offering an aesthetic experience of a piece of nature, especially coming from a post-industrial landscape, could be the first step into thinking about the environment.[2] As a designer, I believe that materials can sometimes speak for themselves, and if these leaves cannot provide scientific evidence, a closer look at them can raise awareness and open up new questions. The herbarium I created is now also part of the Kreismuseum Bitterfeld's collection where the leaves are available for chemical analysis, curious minds and aesthetic experiences.

Pierre Klein

1 Marder, Michael, 'Interview with Michael Marder', in Gibson, Prudence, Brits, Baylee (eds.), *Covert Plants: Vegetal Consciousness and Agency in an Anthropocentric World,* Santa Barbara: Brainstorm Books, 2018, 25–34.
2 Saito, Yuriko, 'Plants and Everyday Aesthetics', in Thorsen, Line Marie (ed.), *Moving Plants, Rønnebæksholm: Narayana Press,* 2017, 35–40.

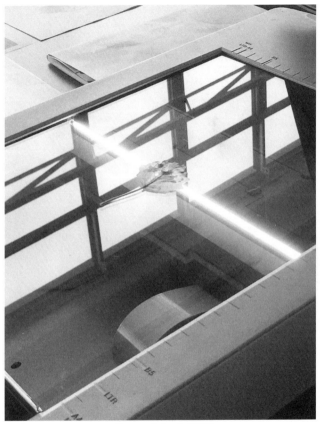

● Scanning process for each leaf, 2021.

● Herbarium of leaves from Bitterfeld collected and pressed by Pierre Klein, now in the Kreismuseum Bitterfeld archive, 2021.

● *Collection d'anomalies*, 2021

Appendix

Vegetation under Power. Infrastructures
Heat! Breath! Growth! Metabolics

The Bauhaus Lab 2021 culminated in an exhibition titled *Vegetation under Power* that presented diverse research topics based on the following keywords: Poetics/Politics, Evidence, Sediments, Traces, Socialities, Recordings, Imprints, Extractions, (Un)rooting, Stewardships and Annotations. While each of these words has a commonly agreed upon meaning, they took on a new form in the context of Bitterfeld's pasts and futures, and brought together the individual insights of each of the Bauhaus Lab 2021's participants.

The lexicon below reveals the meanings these words took on in the context of our research.

● Poetics/Politics – *the interrelation of poetic theory or practice and various forms of political life*
In the context of Bitterfeld, the seemingly inconsequential act of breathing was and is laden with tension and contradiction: the lightness of air and the weight of pollution, its silence and noise, its freedoms and limitations.

● Evidence – *signs or indications of something / information drawn from testimony / the available body of facts or information indicating whether a belief or proposition is true*
The various forms of stains, anomalies and microscopies captured in the records of the Kreismuseum Bitterfeld's archives reflected persistences of the unseen on the brink of being made visible.

● Sediments – *deposits / matter that settles and layers*
An accumulation of temporalities, infrastructures, toxicities and desires. If vegetation and earth-based matter are embroiled in chemical and physical stratifications, they also provide portals for new possibilities.

● Recordings – *made for subsequent reproductions, broadcasts or archives*
Testimonies of situated human encounters with the vegetal otherness.

● Traces – *findings and discoveries resulting from investigation / to follow or mark the course of something with one's eye, mind or finger / to take a particular path or route / to trace a line, outline, map*
Maps and oral testimonies traced the histories of resettled communities, some of which complicated over-simplified narratives of precarity and risk, to locate the lost voices of everyday life in the present.

● Socialities – *the assembling of individuals in communities / the tendency of groups and persons to develop social links and live in communities*
Despite the toxic legacies of heavy environmental degradation, people found ways of living in precarity through systems of care.

● Imprints – *to make impressions upon / to mark / lasting effects*
Imprints of ideologies within a landscape bring forth the interrelations of politics, infrastructure and nature.

- Extractions – *the act or process of drawing forth or pulling out / biological meaning: referring to ancestry or origin*
Carbon cultures have shaped the earth and their implied infrastructures may only be felt in crucial moments of absence or fragility.

- (Un)rooting – *from which something originates or can be obtained / a process by which energy or some other thing enters a system*
The workings of extractive logic and its effects on trees, whether carbonised, fossilised or living, have an effect on humans and non-humans alike.

- Stewardships – *the careful and responsible management of something entrusted to one's care / making wise use of natural resources*
The regime of silence that environmental and political activism fought against has often occluded the distinctions between care and preservation.

- Annotations – *to supply with critical or explanatory notes / completing absences of*
Attempts to question how, and to what degree, conditions in different social, political and economic systems impacted institutionally-bound nature conservation in relation to grass-roots politics.

● *Lili Carr* is an architect with a background in the natural sciences. She holds a diploma from the Architectural Association in London (2016) and a Bachelor of Arts in Physics from the University of Oxford (2009). She is interested in the constructs through which various disciplines perceive, know and tell a place and their impact on spatial design practice. Her work explores the ways in which architectural practice can be attentive to the non-designed effects of the designed spatial transformation it promotes.

● *Maya Errázuriz* is an art historian, curator and editor from Santiago, Chile. Her research focuses on art and ecology applied to nature conservation strategies. She currently works as Head of Art and Publications at the Fundación Mar Adentro, where she leads curatorial research and is in charge of the Bosque Pehuén Residency programme, which seeks to address the conservation of a forest from a trans-disciplinary perspective.

● *Shaiwanti Gupta* is an architect and researcher situating her work on the confluence of rigid industrial systems and the potentials of architectural prowess. She first gained a degree in Architecture, being awarded a Gold Medal, at MNIT Jaipur (2012) before obtaining a Berlage Post-master in Architecture and Urban Design (TU Delft) in 2021. She worked as Deputy Manager Architecture for Engineers India Limited between 2012 and 2019, specialising in petrochemicals, mobility and infrastructure projects for the Government of India.

● *Elizabeth Hong* is a designer whose research-based practice explores raw materials and the traditions, history and culture they embody. Her work focuses on material experimentation as well as the critical reflection of their place in local modes of production and in a circular economy. Combining her social science background with design, she seeks to make visible the connections we share with our natural environment from a social and political perspective.

● *Pierre Klein* is a designer and visual artist based in Paris, France. His work and research highlight elementary phenomena on the edge of perception, playing with colour, space and movement. He conceives alone or with others performances, shows, set displays, exhibitions and micro-editions in which he offers to take a closer look at the ordinary. He teaches design at the Musée des Arts décoratifs in Paris.

● *Elisabetta Rattalino* is an art historian, currently a Postdoctoral Research Fellow at the Free University of Bozen-Bolzano where she teaches Visual Culture. Her research engages with artistic practices and visual and design cultures from 1945 to present day, with a focus on rural environments and landscapes.

● *Shivani Shedde* is an architect and doctoral candidate in the History and Theory of Architecture at Princeton University. Her research includes the spatial imperatives of colonial mapping, visualisation and governance techniques, the politics of extraction and its relationship with architectural materials, as well as the effects of mass decolonisation in the 1960s – in particular, the various south-to-south solidarity movements – that shaped discourses concerning architecture and the value of dissent.

● *Nancy Dayanne Valladares* is an interdisciplinary artist and filmmaker from Tegucigalpa, Honduras. Her work grapples with the constructions of vegetal imaginaries and the spectres that lie within. Her image-based practice delves into the formation of optical tools and their accompanying visual regimes. Nancy's practice closely examines photography's historical entanglement with botanical imaginaries and chemical legacies.

● Ornithology exhibition in the Kreismuseum Bitterfeld, 1976.

● Bauhaus Taschenbuch 26
The book is published in the context of the Bauhaus Lab
2021 exhibition presented at the Bauhaus Dessau from
9 December 2021 to 2 February 2022 and in the Kreismuseum Bitterfeld from 2 March to 31 July 2022.

● Edited by
Bauhaus Dessau Foundation
Director Dr. Barbara Steiner
Gropiusallee 38
06846 Dessau-Roßlau
Telephone +49-340-6508-250
www.bauhaus-dessau.de

● Academy Team, Bauhaus Dessau Foundation:
Programme head: Dr. Regina Bittner
Research associate: Philipp Sack
Student assistant: Lisa Thiel

● Bauhaus Lab 2021 participants: Lili Carr, Maya Errázuriz,
Shaiwanti Gupta, Pierre Klein, Elizabeth Hong, Elisabetta
Rattalino, Shivani Shedde and Nancy Dayanne Valladares.

● Editing
Maya Errázuriz, Elisabetta Rattalino, Shivani Shedde

● Translation and Copyediting
Bauhaus Lab 2021
Petra Frese
Rebecca Philipps Williams

● Project management
Katja Klaus

● Graphic design
Anne Meyer
based on a concept by HORT, Berlin
www.hort.org.uk

● Printed by
Pöge Druck, Leipzig
www.poegedruck.de

● Publisher
Spector Books, Leipzig
www.spectorbooks.com

● Distribution
Germany, Austria: GVA, Gemeinsame Verlagsauslieferung
Göttingen GmbH & Co. KG,
www.gva-verlage.de
Switzerland: AVA Verlagsauslieferung AG, www.ava.ch
France, Belgium: Interart Paris, www.interart.fr
UK: Central Books Ltd, www.centralbooks.com
USA, Canada, Central and South America, Africa
ARTBOOK | D.A.P. www.artbook.com
Japan: twelvebooks, www.twelve-books.com
South Korea: The Book Society, www.thebooksociety.org
Australia, New Zealand: Perimeter Distribution,
www.perimeterdistribution.com

Vegetation under Power is the result of the research carried out by the participants of the Bauhaus Lab 2021 programme, a three-month research programme of the Bauhaus Dessau Foundation.

The programme's final presentation was accompanied by an international symposium which took place on 9 December 2021 in a hybrid format. Here, the participants invited experts to discuss questions of new nature-culture relations, the knowledge of herbaria, the politics of the environment and the anthropology of infrastructures with Lucia Pietroiusti (UK), Michael Marder (Spain), Kenny Cupers (Switzerland) and Caroline Ektander (Sweden).

We would like to thank the following persons, institutions and archives for their contributions and generous support: Yvonne Tenschert, Henning Seilkopf, Sebastian Czerny, Cora Proeschold, Katarina Neurer, Tom Dietrich, Julia Schäfer, Martha Schwindling, Stefania Rigoni, Yon González de Matauko, Mauricio Sosa Noreña, Martin Brück, Fred Walkow, Heidi Karstedt, Jonas Venediger, Martina Schön, Ingo Brämer, Rosi Topf, Roland Hermann, Kreismuseum Bitterfeld archive, Bauhaus Dessau Foundation Archive, Robert Havemann Gesellschaft, Bauhaus Dessau Foundation Library, Ferropolis, Kraftwerk Zschornewitz, Osten Festival.

First edition, 2022
© Bauhaus Dessau Foundation
ISBN 978-3-95905-587-1

The Bauhaus Dessau Foundation is a non-profit foundation under public law. It is institutionally funded by:

 Die Beauftragte der Bundesregierung für Kultur und Medien

SACHSEN-ANHALT

Dessau
⌐ Roßlau

Additionally, the Bauhaus Lab 2021 was supported by:

**creative industries
fund NL**

● p. 40
© Maya Errázuriz, 2021

● p. 43
Diagram showing oil-based by-products derived from coal, diagram from p. 7 of R. H. Francé's book *Lebender Braunkohlenwald,* 1932.

● p. 44, 45
Coal Intimacies by Shaiwanti Gupta, 2021. Illustration mapping the kitchen products derived from the coal and chemical industries.

● p. 46, 47
Working women at the Agfa Film Factory, 1950–1960.
© Kreismuseum Bitterfeld archive

● p. 53
© Kreismuseum Bitterfeld archive

● p. 56, 57
Exercise for the exhibition *Spur der Kohlen* by Bauhaus Dessau student Oliver Blomeier, 1993.
© Oliver Blomeier, Bauhaus Dessau

● p. 58
Items in the Kreismuseum Bitterfeld archive.
© Maya Errázuriz, 2021

● p. 61
A selection of the Naturschutzwochen posters from the Kreismuseum Bitterfeld archive presented in the exhibition *Vegetation under Power*. © Bauhaus Dessau Foundation / Photo: Meyer, Thomas, 2021 / OSTKREUZ

● p. 63
Hot air balloon advertises Bitterfeld's Umweltbibliothek. Image featured in the *Bitterfelder Zeitung,* August 1993. Original Photo: Andreas Stedtler.

● p. 65
Images of Comrade Nikita Khrushchev's visit to Bitterfeld during the 5th congress of the Socialist Unity Party of Germany in the GDR. This visit was followed by the 1959 Bitterfelder Konferenz, a conference held at the Kultur-palast Bitterfeld. © Kreismuseum Bitterfeld archive

● p. 66, 67
Soviet soldiers help to lay tracks in a lignite open-cast mine, Bitterfeld 1977
© René Bär, Kreismuseum Bitterfeld archive 11203

● p. 77
Plant fossils were common by-products of the coal mining industry, imprints of the cyclical metabolisms of the earth. Photo from the Deutsches Bergbau-Museum Bochum, 2021. © Nancy Dayanne Valladares

● p. 78
The kaleidoscopic surface of a brown coal briquette as seen through an electron microscope. Still from the short film *Herbarium,* 2021. © Nancy Dayanne Valladares

● p. 80
Machinery producing film at the Agfa-Orwo Film Factory (now the Industrie- und Filmmuseum Wolfen).
© Nancy Dayanne Valladares, 2022

● p. 83
Photographic experiment: A solution of sodium hypochlorite dissolves the layers of photographic emulsion on black-and-white sheet film. © Nancy Dayanne Valladares, 2022

● p. 87
VEB Braunkohlenwerk map of open-cast mines and railway systems outlined on a map of Saxony-Anhalt, 1987.
© Kreismuseum Bitterfeld archive

● p. 88
The Golpa-Nord open-cast mine
© Kreismuseum Bitterfeld archive

● p. 97
Frontispiece of Werner Rothmaler's *Exkursionsflora von Deutschland*, 1962, annotated by Ms. Einenkel.
© Kreismuseum Bitterfeld archive

● p. 99
Peter Feige, herbarium sheet *(Galanthus nivalis),* 1949.
© Kreismuseum Bitterfeld archive

● p. 100
Emil Obst, herbarium sheet (multiple species), ca. 1918.
© Kreismuseum Bitterfeld archive

● p. 102
Woman collecting snowdrops in the Goitzsche, 1922,
photographer unknown. © Kreismuseum Bitterfeld archive

● p. 104
Ruth Hollós-Consemüller, untitled (Snowdrops),
1920/1929, Bauhaus Dessau Foundation (I 44716) /
© (Hollos-Consemüller, Ruth) Consemüller, Stephan.

● p. 107
Hans Weber's herbarium, *Ulmus montana Withering*, 1930.
© Kreismuseum Bitterfeld archive

● p. 108
Collecting leaves in Bitterfeld, 2021. © Pierre Klein

● p. 111
Scanning process for each leaf, 2021. © Pierre Klein

● p. 112
Herbarium of leaves from Bitterfeld collected and pressed by
Pierre Klein, now in the Kreismuseum Bitterfeld archive, 2021.

● p. 113
Collection d'anomalies, 2021 © Pierre Klein

● p. 123
Ornithology exhibition in the Kreismuseum Bitterfeld
© Kreismuseum Bitterfeld archive

● Front page
© Kreismuseum Bitterfeld archive

● Exhibition photos p. 14–25
Bauhaus Dessau Foundation
© Thomas Meyer / OSTKREUZ, 2021

● Exhibition photo p. 26–27
Bauhaus Dessau Foundation
© Philipp Sack

● Bauhaus Taschenbuch 2
Architektur aus der Schuhbox.
Baťas internationale Fabrikstädte

● Bauhaus Taschenbuch 3
Kibbuz und Bauhaus. Pioniere des Kollektivs

● Bauhaus Taschenbuch 5
Das Bauhausgebäude in Dessau
The Bauhaus building in Dessau

● Bauhaus Taschenbuch 6
Vom Bauhaus nach Palästina.
Chanan Frenkel, Ricarda und Heinz Schwerin

● Bauhaus Taschenbuch 7
Die Siedlung Dessau-Törten 1926 bis 1931

● Bauhaus Taschenbuch 9
Die unsichtbare Bauhausstadt. Eine Spurensuche
in Dessau

● Bauhaus Taschenbuch 11
Junges Design am Bauhaus Dessau

● Bauhaus Taschenbuch 12
Bauhaus Lab 2013. Architecture after Speculation

● Bauhaus Taschenbuch 14
Die Werkbundsiedlung Stuttgart Weissenhof